First Among Beautiful Stars

A Poetry Chapbook

by

emmett wheatfall

Cover infrared view of the Horsehead Nebula
Hubble's 23rd anniversary image

Frontispiece "Eclipse" by Sebastian Voltmer

Graphic design by Dale Champlin

Author photo by

Published by
Just a Lark Books
308 SE Walnut Street

JUST A LARK BOOKS
Hillsboro, Oregon

Body copy set in Garamond Pro

First edition

10 9 8 7 6 5 4 3 2 1

ISBN 9798892175647

For Annie Lighthart,

whose poetry workshops will forever be

an inspiration accompanying my poetic journey.

A wise man doesn't say everything he thinks

but thinks every single thing he says.

Rumi

TABLE OF CONTENTS

First Among Beautiful Stars

First Among Beautiful Stars

First Among Beautiful Stars

I shudder to think about returning to the deep

To that vast oasis of darkness lacking beautiful stars

To that subconscious world where absent are continents

Will I again know myself, let alone my given name

All I've ever known is the temporal light of life

If there is the light of God, let Him illuminate me

So that I be first among beautiful stars

Ever So Grand

Humans are small

    Tiny creatures

Pinky fingers in creation

    Possessing peacock arrogance

Among things ever so grand

Like the universe

    And its many galaxies

Bright white stars

    Light golden moon and sun

Indomitable oceans and seas

These are ever so grand

    Overshadowing humanity

Humans being tiny creatures

    Never smashed under a shoe

Rinsed away by rainwater

Observed as inferior

    Howbeit, crown jewel of all

Fashioned in God's likeness

    Who is neither big nor small

Bad Mama Jamma

You meant more to me than you
Your sudden passing that was
                Your cough was pretty bad
Was petty an oxymoron for bad
Or was the inverse just as unruly

        Among stars you were starlit
        Often called a Bad Mama Jamma
                Now you will never be more
        In the world to come all that
You mean more to me than you

A Metaphor for Conception

A star born

Doesn't know it

Its universe does

A fetus conceived

Doesn't know it

Its mother does

And to That End

To begin with, I will spin this the way a Black Widow Spider would. Messy, yet, for certain. In the insolent inner eyes of your human imagination, it won't appear plausible. And to your cavernous and evacuated ears be a fair-minded fool. So, with all earnestness— observe and listen. For your neo-imagination is a neon light seized upon by starlit nights. And to that end, be sure not to miss watching wolves howling at the blood red moon.

Of the Divine

Summer evenings /

sitting in my living room /

front door open /

screen door locked /

with the lights off /

night moonlit /

shadow casting /

my world quiet within /

and the stars beyond /

being of the divine /

I find sanctuary /

Poets *v* Stars

Are there more poets than stars

Certainly not says the full moon

As a subtle fog rolls itself inland

Poets everywhere continue writing

Illuminated Verse

Never think to criticize creation

Your eraser is not big enough

Revel not about Milky Way candy bars

Wait until you've visited the Milky Way

The universe is certainly big

Bigger is illuminated verse by Billy Collins

If you do not appreciate gravity

Try understanding the gravity of any matter

Gene Roddenberry was a visionary

Janus is the doorkeeper to the heavens

Among the stars are brave new worlds

On earth many stars have fallen

Humanity must push the bounds of existence

Boldly go! where not thought possible

If human existence is one dimensional

Two-dimensional thinking might hold promise

Why reach for the stars

Is there anything beyond human grasp

My Muse

Where is my boyfriend

Ah! That's right. I don't have one

I'm not a girl. I think I know that

Amusing myself with the notion

    I ponder

What if I were one? A girl that is

One among of beautiful girls

One among fairer looking girls

One longing to be similarly stipulated

One captured in boys' eyes

One twinkling like girl stars

In the secret chamber of a girl's heart

Swayed by her tender emotions

Led round and about like soft wind

Spun up like unraked leaves

    I

Have strayed in my thinking

That I had a boyfriend

Not understanding that I don't

Need a boy to have boyfriend

Many boys are my boyfriend

Must I bifurcate boyfriend

Are they not one in the same

I am a friend to many boys

Am I a boyfriend to them

Or am I their boyfriend instead

This is my musing

In Solemn Contempt

I will spot you the moments

Seed you the rest of my days

If only you would love

The very best of me

And the worst of me

In solemn contempt

For in that manner in due course

I will know I am the one

The one fairer than your mother

Never the toss up of a two-sided coin

With heads being the tale told

And tails the sins never repeated

I will spot the moments

Seed you the rest of my days

Notice you among beautiful stars

If only you would love

The very best of me

And the worst of me

In solemn contempt

Shining High Among the Stars

It had never been his turn to dance, his wheelchair

wanted to anyway, the way a wheel spins on a spindle.

How many of us have experienced a flat tire, had our

breath taken away by faded roses, lost a

tennis shoe at the height of a run? There is space for

him on the dance floor. All the pretty girls

wearing ruby red lipstick and perfectly pink cheeks, hiked skirts,

stand ready to spin him into a newfound frenzy.

The earth is a difficult place to escape, given the

relative awareness of gravity. It's the memorable moments,

them being few and far between. For one night

and one moment, I imagine he felt like he had walked.

And the moon, shining high among the stars, went

from being a half-moon to a full one.

Teddy Bear Imprinted Pajamas

Where do the many beautiful stars come from

Breakfast cereal makers should FedEx them back

Jumbo transport planes ascend to a max 43,000 feet

Just shy of the translucent hem above the earth

Ask any flock of birds and wait for their winked eye

Knowing its silly thinking heaven is ascendable

Gazing into this morning's bowl of breakfast cereal

How amazed I am at the spooned milk drenched stars

I know I am luckier than all the astronauts in space

All they can do is peer at stars through glass portals

This kid not only sees stars but can taste them too

And Grade-A homogenized milk is their angel dust

This whole experience feels comically cosmic

These teddy bear imprinted pajamas are my space suit

My bare feet feel like they're dangling over earth's edge

Only fools would dare say the earth is not flat

Twinkling in Their Eyes

I fell in love with a French woman /

younger than me / I was predisposed /

What I learned is that doves do fly /

Far above earthly plain / At night /

They see stars / Twinkling in their eyes /

Not Another Hand

from the pitched black of darkness

there arose a black hand

it belonged to wicked white men

who severed it at sea

from the pitch black of darkness

there rose other black hands

belonging to other wicked white men

who severed them

why didn't the clouds

let beautiful stars cover their eyes

and blackness of seas

welcome them like naive children

and burgeoning wind finding

tethered reasons for torment

ship manifests held no names

for any of the black hands

curse words flew at

nameless black men and women

while the sea did not billow

and slave ships did not bellow

chains did rattle

and stocks held securely their lock

to the pitched black of darkness

black hands returned

from the pitched black of darkness

there rose not another hand

given how the dirt covered graves

of white men bear invisible crosses

Pixie Dust in Our Eyes

If in the absence of flowers,

then what? A question mark (?).

How about an asterisk (*)?

Will sunshiny days return?

Will blue sky conjure up?

If not, why? Why point then to the

stars, trim stubble from the moon's

beard, toss pixie dust before our eyes?

Dare I suggest we smile awhile,

whisper into a seashell's ear,

then wait for a reply? Why? I'm

left to wonder. And you?

More Darkness Will Come

Without rebellion comes the night

Fortunately, it bears no shining armor

No glimmering of beautiful stars

Darker the berry better the juice

Deeper the darkness greater is the light

Light illuminates this room

Neither has retrieved its sword

Unsheathed from sleeve its cutlery

Not a sentinel intervenes

As has been the turn of the centuries

I rub my eyes and new darkness appears

When I fall asleep more darkness will come

I fear the dark and am drawn to light

These two are metaphors for something

What that is I do not know

Neither do I take them ever-so lightly

Beyond the Edge of Earth

Time immeasurable. Mine, the longest length on my palm.

It has never been read. Dead is my mother. So too is my father.

The sun sets every evening. How far away is west?

I'm watching the sun travel an ocean's length to settle somewhere

beyond the edge of the earth. It is a warm night on this sandy beach.

Clusters of beautiful stars appear distant. If only I could retrieve one

like I do a bowl of Trix cereal. Momma, I know milk must last.

Why call me a greedy? Time is immeasurable.

In *First Among Beautiful Stars*, Emmett Wheatfall writes
"If there is the light of God, let Him illuminate me / So I be
first among the beautiful stars." Wheatfall is a stargazer. This
chapbook is beautiful, mystical, and spiritual. He invites the
reader to experience awe, wonderment, and a sense of oneness.
He insists what comes in darkness becomes light. Wheatfall
finds sanctuary in his stargazing. "And the moon, shining high
among the stars, went / from being half-moon to a full one."

Sherri Levine, Poet
Author of *Stealing Flowers from the Neighbors*

Author Bio

Emmett Wheatfall lives in Portland, Oregon. He writes, records, publishes, features, and performs poetry to music. Fernwood Press, an imprint of Barclay Press has published three books of Emmett's poetry. His collection titled *As Clean as a Bone* was published in May 2018. *As Clean as a Bone* was a 2019 Eric Hoffer Award Finalist as well as a da Vinci Eye award finalist. *Our Scarlet Blue Wounds* was published in November 2019. *Our Scarlet Blue Wounds* examines poetically American "Exceptionalism" in light of political, social, and economic constructs. *With Extreme Prejudice, Lest We Forget* addresses poetically on the worldwide COVID-19 pandemic. It was published in May 2022.

9 798892 175647